THE MOON OF THE
ALLIGATORS

THE THIRTEEN MOONS

The Moon of the Owls (JANUARY)

The Moon of the Bears (FEBRUARY)

The Moon of the Salamanders (MARCH)

The Moon of the Chickarees (APRIL)

The Moon of the Monarch Butterflies (MAY)

The Moon of the Fox Pups (JUNE)

The Moon of the Wild Pigs (JULY)

The Moon of the Mountain Lions (AUGUST)

The Moon of the Deer (SEPTEMBER)

The Moon of the Alligators (OCTOBER)

The Moon of the Gray Wolves (NOVEMBER)

The Moon of the Winter Bird (DECEMBER)

The Moon of the Moles (DECEMBER-JANUARY)

THE MOON OF THE
ALLIGATORS

BY JEAN CRAIGHEAD GEORGE

ILLUSTRATED BY MICHAEL ROTHMAN

HarperCollins*Publishers*

The Moon of the Alligators
Text copyright © 1969, 1991 by Jean Craighead George
Illustrations copyright © 1991 by Michael Rothman
Typography by Al Cetta
1 2 3 4 5 6 7 8 9 10
NEW EDITION

Library of Congress Cataloging-in-Publication Data
George, Jean Craighead, date
    The moon of the alligators / by Jean Craighead George ; illustrated
by Michael Rothman.—New ed.
        p.   cm. — (The Thirteen moons)
    Includes bibliographical references and index.
    Summary: Describes an alligator's desperate search for food in the
Florida Everglades during the month of October.
    ISBN 0-06-022427-4. — ISBN 0-06-022428-2 (lib. bdg.)
    1. Alligators—Florida—Everglades—Juvenile literature.
[1. Alligators—Florida—Everglades.]   I. Rothman, Michael, ill.
II. Title.   III. Series: George, Jean Craighead, date,   Thirteen
moons.
QL795.A4G46   1991   90-38169
597.98—dc20   CIP
                                                                   AC

Why is this series called The Thirteen Moons?

Each year there are either thirteen full moons or thirteen new moons. This series of books is named in their honor.

Our culture, which bases its calendar on sun-time, has no names for the thirteen moons. I have named the thirteen lunar months after thirteen North American animals. Primarily night prowlers, these animals, at a particular time of the year in a particular place, do wondrous things. The places are known to you, but the animal moon names are not because I made them up. So that you can place them on our sun calendar, I have identified them with the names of our months. When I ran out of these, I gave the thirteenth moon, the Moon of the Moles, the expandable name December-January.

Fortunately, the animals do not need calendars, for names or no names, sun-time or moon-time, they follow their own inner clocks.

—JEAN CRAIGHEAD GEORGE

TWO EYES POKED ABOVE THE STILL water. Each iris was silver-yellow and each pupil black and narrow. They were the eyes of the alligator of Sawgrass Hole, who was floating like a log on the surface of the water as she watched for food. She saw the blue sky above her, and because her eyes were on the top and to the rear of her head, she saw all the way behind her to the tall cypress trees. Their limbs spread like silver wires above a tangle of sweet bay and buttonbushes.

The alligator did not move, but watched and

waited even though hunger gnawed her belly. She had eaten little since June, when the rainy season had flooded her home and the prey she fed upon had swum away. Now her sense of seasonal rhythm told her that the afternoon's cloudless sky meant the end of the rains and hurricanes, and the return of the wildlife to her water hole. The moon of October was the beginning of southern Florida's dry season. The water level would fall. The fish, frogs, turtles, and birds would come back to Sawgrass Hole, where she lived. They would be followed by the herons and ibis, egrets, anhinga or water turkeys, and she would eat well once more.

She was in her pool in the Everglades of Florida, which is not a swamp as it is often called, but a river like none other in the world. The Everglades does not flow—it seeps. Forty to sixty miles wide and a hundred miles long, it creeps, like glistening quicksilver, from Lake Okeechobee southward across a flat limestone bed to the

Florida Bay. The Everglades is not only a river, but also a wet prairie. Saw grass, that rugged plant whose grasslike leaves are edged with sharp spines, grows like a crop from shore to shore. Rising out of the saw grass are tree islands, known as hammocks, where a variety of trees grow. Other islands are forests of bay, called "heads," buttonwood and cypress trees.

The Everglades and its plants and creatures, including the alligator, have adapted to the wet and dry seasons of the semitropical zone in south Florida. When the river is high in summer's wet season, little fish, like guppies and gambusia that eat mosquito larvae, swim among the saw grass stalks far out in the river. They dodge the largemouth bass and sunfish, who, in turn, avoid the Florida soft-shelled turtle.

During the winter season when the river is low, the wildlife of the Everglades adjusts to dryness. As the water level drops, and just before the river bottom becomes exposed to the sun and cracks, the river creatures come to the alligator holes. They live through the drought of winter in these watery sanctuaries.

October was always a critical time for the alligators as they waited for their food to return. In this century, however, the month of October has become a near disaster for them. Human-made canals, dug into the limestone to drain the Everglades for farming, have killed off millions and billions of frogs, fish, birds, mammals, and turtles. Their food depleted, the alligators died in huge numbers from starvation. In addition, hunters killed tens of thousands for their valuable skins. The passing of the alligators threatened all the wildlife in the Everglades, for their holes are oases for life during the dry season. The great flocks of beautiful birds were reduced to a few. Fish and turtles died out for lack of winter retreats. The alligator, people began to realize, was the "farmer" that kept the chain of life going.

In the 1970s there were so few American alligators left on this earth that Congress declared it an endangered species, one that is doomed to extinction and would be protected by law. Since that decree, the big reptiles have made a strong comeback in their original homeland that stretches from Texas to North Carolina. They are now only a threatened species.

The six-foot alligator of Sawgrass Hole did not know about her status, she only knew her belly ached. Sinking to the bottom of the pool, she looked for food. The river was getting low. A few minnows too small to bother with darted past her. A measly pollywog rested in the warm mud. She ignored it, whipped her tail from side to side, and then circled her large home. The water was filling with algae, one-celled plants that grow profusely in the sun. Long strips of these green plants floated in scummy masses. They bothered her.

With a powerful thrust from her tail she drove her body into a patch of algae and caught it on her nose. Swimming with surprising grace, she carried it to the shore and pushed it up with her nose and feet, then returned and bulldozed another load ashore. Next she went to the overgrown water lilies floating on the surface. Taking a plant in her mouth, she tugged it across the pool and dragged it up on land to die.

When she was done she could see the minnows more clearly, and the minnows, freed from the weeds, flickered back and forth across Sawgrass Hole eating microscopic food called periphyton. In the days that followed, they grew rapidly and larger fish fed on them. For the alligator, however, there was no food big enough for her to bother with.

Her hole, which was fifteen feet deep and some forty feet long and wide, was far out in the Everglades at the edge of a cypress head. On one of its shores was a beach where she sunbathed. Around the edges of the pool in the shallow water grew pickerelweed and arrowheads. Among their stems the fry of the largemouth bass grew up. On the shore, just out of the water, grew clumps of six-foot-tall alligator flags. Their large leaves, on the ends of long stalks, waved and fluttered like banners. These plants announce the locations of alligator homes to human, bird, and beast. When the big reptiles are killed or die, the plants die too, for there is no alligator-farmer to weed. The algae multiply and clog the pools, weeds take over the shallows and shore and, finally, trees and bushes fill in the pond, choking out the alligator flags.

One evening the big 'gator lay near the shore watching the bushes. The moon of October was working its change. The water in the river was lowering, and the fish and wildlife were coming to her deep hole. A snowy egret alighted

on a limb of a pop ash near the water. The bird no longer held his feathers close to his body as he did in summer, but lifted them slightly to let his delicate plumes float down the back of his neck like a veil. The moon of October is the beginning of the breeding season for the egrets. In a month or so he would strut for his mate, spread his plumes, then bow and dance for her.

The egret picked up a stick, held it a moment, then dropped it. It was a present for his mate, but he was not quite ready to give it to her. October was a time to practice the art of courtship, and practice he did. He picked up another stick. The alligator eyed him but did not stalk. He was too high in the tree to catch.

The bird flew, his yellow feet and black legs gleaming as he skimmed over Sawgrass Hole and climbed into the air. High over the 'gator hole, he turned and headed for his rookery on a buttonwood island near the Florida Bay. The 'gator watched him until he was out of sight, then submerged herself in the river. She made no ripples to alarm her prey, nor did she disturb the waters as she pressed her huge jaws together. They closed over seventy sharp white teeth, forming the perpetual grin of an alligator. Her tail, almost half of her length, torpedoed her across the pool to the shore where the cypress trees grew. As she came up on land, water spilled from her sculptured armor and her third eyelid pulled back to let her see in the air.

The alligator saw movement beneath a pop ash. Rising to her feet on short legs, she peered into a brushy jungle that she and her ancestors had created. For a thousand years the alligators of Sawgrass Hole had made land by weeding and piling the debris on this shore. Tree seeds had rooted in the rich compost. The seedlings had grown into a sheltering jungle that attracted rabbits, raccoons, bobcats, and river otter.

The 'gator lunged at a marsh rabbit who was nibbling on leaves. He had been born in late summer. With the rise of the moon of October he had left home to seek his fortune. He had not gone far before he came upon the alligator's jungle and, finding it rich with rabbit food, settled in. Blackish-brown in color, he looked like the cottontail rabbits of the north, except that he had no white on his tail. However, he did possess their ability to leap, and before the alligator could lunge a second time, he had catapulted over her tail and plunged into the pool. He swam quickly across Sawgrass Hole and bounced ashore. Marsh rabbits are excellent swimmers.

Being so close to catching a rabbit made the alligator even hungrier. She dove into her pool and scanned the undersides of the bladderworts, floating plants that catch insects and take nourishment from them. No dark areas marked the bodies of resting frogs. They were still out in the glades. Patiently she waited.

Days passed. Her hunger increased.

One morning she crawled onto her sunny beach to warm her muscles. The nights were cooler now, and since alligators are cold-blooded animals, she depended on the sun to warm her up. After basking for an hour she started off into the saw grass to look for food. The trail she took was as old as her pool. A raised roadbed, it consisted of dead saw grass, trampled by generations of alligators traveling from Sawgrass Hole to the glades and islands. The path was used heavily. In April the bull alligators from tens of miles around came down it to breed the females of Sawgrass Hole. In summer and fall when food was scarce the females and young walked the path to hammocks and moats.

The alligator moved more slowly on land than in water, yet she covered the mile to the edge of her territory long before noon. Hunger was driving her swiftly to the hardwood hammock to hunt.

Hammocks are not like any other islands. They are greenhouses on rock outcrops in the "river of grass," and they are mysteriously beautiful. Handsome hardwood trees, live oaks, gumbo-limbos, mastics, and mahoganies grow there. Orchids, air plants, ferns, and mosses festoon the tree limbs and trunks. Since no drying winds penetrate the dense canopy of the hammocks, the air inside is moist and warm, as in a greenhouse, and the plants grow in profusion.

The alligator climbed ashore. She pushed between red maples and pop ashes at the edge of the hammock and entered a large, dimly lit forest. A bobcat was sleeping on the broad limb of a live oak. He did not run when he saw the alligator, nor did she when she saw the cat. Bobcats and big alligators have no enemies but humans.

She rounded a mossy log and came to a stop.

Her reptilian memory recognized a limb of the live oak above her and warned her of an old disaster. She lay still.

The fear passed and she walked on. Within a few feet she saw the greenish-yellow flowers of the butterfly orchid. A warning bell rang in her brain and again she stopped. Cautiously she looked around. A snow-white ghost orchid bloomed at her side. She recalled having seen that before too. The grass ferns that hung from a sable palm like a beard were also familiar. On a log the resurrection ferns, now curling up to live out the dry season, warned her to go back. Once she had met trouble here. She stopped her trek.

Hunger overcame her fear and she started off again. A flock of warblers dropped down from the canopy where they had been feeding and flew over the pineapplelike bromeliads on the ground. The little birds were migrating from New England and Canada to Mexico and South

America. Every October they stopped in the hammocks of the Everglades to feed on the abundant insects. The presence of the warblers also sent a message of warning to the alligator, but she was painfully hungry.

She walked toward a deep hole she remembered. It was one of the many holes in the Everglades leached out of the limestone by the acids from decaying plants. They are called solution holes. This one was twenty feet across, fifteen feet deep, round and straight-sided like a well. It was filled with water to its fern-trimmed top. In its depths swam huge garfish. When they were very small, they had entered the solution hole through Swiss cheese-like openings that pock the limestone. Then they had grown too big to swim out. The alligator saw them, but hesitated to dive into the hole. A fuzzy memory held her back.

The sun went down suddenly as it does in the

semitropics and the big reptile lay still. Her upper and lower lids closed over her bright eyes and she slept.

The moon came up. The raccoons walked up and down tree limbs catching tree frogs. Some romped along the water edge hunting for crayfish. The bobcat awoke and continued his solitary trek across the October glades. He had left his mother and his brother a year ago, and would live alone until late December, when he would find a female of his choice and mate. He would not stay with her long, for like most cats, he was a solitary animal.

At dawn the alligator looked into the solution hole again, and again she did not dive in. Her reptilian mind was clicking off memories of another October when she had been younger.

Her life had begun in August buried under a pile of warm, decaying vegetation near Sawgrass Hole. The mound, a nest, was eight to ten feet

wide and five feet high. Even while she was still inside her egg, the baby alligator heard her mother grunting and calling to her. With great effort, she struggled out of her brittle eggshell and clawed her way up through the debris toward the sound. As she neared the surface, her mother's scaly foot gently pulled back the vegetation, and the baby alligator scrambled into August's steamy heat. She was eight inches long.

She was joined by thirty-nine other baby alligators, who, like herself, looked exactly like their parents, except for their round knobby heads and the bright-yellow spots on the end of each body scale. Full of spirit, the babies began to snap at each other as they ran to their grunting mother. When all were free of the nest, she led them toward the water as fast as she was able. Baby alligators have many enemies.

Even on that first day of life the hatchling alligator was a survivor. Sensing danger, she

marched under the protection of her mother's jaw. This was wise. No sooner had she and her tribe reached the trail to Sawgrass Hole than a great blue heron dropped out of the sky. He ate two babies before their mother could grab him in her teeth. Then swiftly, as if word of the hatchlings had been broadcast across the Everglades, the herons and hawks arrived to prey on them. A black snake slipped down a live oak tree, snatched one and swallowed it. A raccoon, hearing the mother alligator grunting and the birds screaming, came down from the same tree and grabbed a straggler.

When the baby alligator reached Sawgrass Hole there were only twenty-three of the forty alive. Since she was one of them, she continued to stay close to her mother. She entered the water under her jaw and stayed there while the lively flotilla of big and little 'gators crossed the pond. Bright flecks of sunlight danced on the surface of the

water and strange water beetles scooted past her.

Tiny fish darted by. Instinctively the baby snapped at them, but did not come out from under her mother. She stayed right where she was until they reached a cave. It had been chewed, clawed, and scraped into existence by the female alligators of Sawgrass Hole to protect their babies from predators. The little alligator scrambled out of the water and lay down on a narrow beach far back in the cave. She was very tired.

For the next nine months the baby 'gator swam in and out of the cave catching minnows and bugs. She ate well and avoided her enemies. By April she was eighteen inches long and too big for the predators to attack her.

Nevertheless she stayed with her mother until another year passed. One day a huge bull 'gator came to Sawgrass Hole. He swam, rolled, and splashed with her mother. He bellowed mating cries that could be heard a mile away. After a few weeks he departed and the alligator's mother was no longer friendly to her. She attacked her now three-foot-long daughter frequently. One night she drove her out of Sawgrass Hole. The mother's loyalty lay with a new clutch of eggs in a new nest.

The young alligator followed the family trail through the saw grass and moved into a moat at the edge of the very hammock she was on now. She felt the river rise and watched the fish and turtles swim away. Food became scarce. Then October came and the river began to drop. One afternoon the alligator went into the hammock to hunt. She walked beneath the orchids and the mahogany trees, she saw the warblers, passed the butterfly orchid and discovered the solution hole. It was filled with trapped fish. Without hesitating, she splashed into its waters and before sunset was full and content.

For a month she lived well on the garfish.

Then, out of food, restless to move on, she tried to climb out. She could not. The water had dropped too low; the steep sides of the solution hole were impossible to climb.

The alligator was trapped. She saw the warblers leave, she saw the air plants bloom on the live oak limb overhead, and she saw the world above her grow smaller and smaller as the water dropped her deeper and deeper into the dark pit. Finally, only the tip of the oak limb was visible above her, and she was on the dry bottom of the solution hole without food or water.

By spring she was starving to death. Then one night a marsh rabbit, who was running away from a bobcat, fell into the hole. Several weeks later an armadillo tumbled down to her. Deep in the solution hole, the young alligator existed on chance while stoically waiting for life or death.

June brought the rains back. Clouds gathered, lightning flashed, and torrents fell from dark

thunderheads. The solution hole began to fill with water. One day a veritable deluge of rain poured into the hole and lifted her to the top. Mustering what little energy she had left, she crawled out of her prison and dragged herself home to Sawgrass Hole.

When she had reached her home, she paused. Something was wrong. Algae and weeds filled her pool. The alligator flags were dead. The once-clear water was green. Snapping turtles haunted the murky depths, for there were no alligators in Sawgrass Hole to keep them in check. Human poachers had found the ancestral home and killed all the magnificent reptiles.

The young alligator went to work. Eagerly she ate the turtles and weeded the pond. The fish returned, the birds came to eat the fish, and the mammals arrived to catch the birds. When Sawgrass Hole was clear of weeds, the alligator flags again brightened its edges with their flashy leaves.

That had been three years ago. Now on the edge of that same solution hole, the alligator was remembering, in her reptilian way, that she should not go after the fish. Torn between her terrible hunger and her sense of survival, she simply lay still. That evening a family of raccoons approached the hole. She lunged at them. Three jumped into the solution hole, swam and climbed safely out. A fourth ran down the trail, with the alligator lumbering after it. Although she could move as swiftly as a closing switchblade when she was close to an animal, she was no match for a running raccoon.

And now, since she faced homeward, she kept on going. She pushed between the red maples, swam across the moat, and took the ancestral trail to Sawgrass Hole.

She slid into the water. Even in her short absence things had changed. The water had dropped three inches. Large patches of algae had died and taken oxygen from the water as they decayed. Hundreds of minnows had suffocated.

Once more the alligator went to work—dragging, pushing, and bulldozing weeds to let the sunlight into her pool. This year there were no big turtles to eat and her hunger increased.

When the moon arose at the end of October, her home was ready to receive the migrants from the drying river. Her pool sparkled. Presently little bass and garfish wiggled into the clear water through holes in the limestone. Snails became abundant at the edge of Sawgrass Hole as they sought the stems of the moist plants that grew there.

Three egrets came to the pond to fish in the shallows. The following afternoon five arrived, then twenty-five. Behind them many big turtles were plodding slowly toward the fresh water. Purple gallinules arrived to eat the water beetles, and the bobcat came in to eat the gallinules. Little fish ate the microscopic creatures of the pond, big fish ate little fish, and the alligator would eat the big fish.

When the moon of October was waning, the leaves of the cypress began to fall. The foliage of the persimmon and maple trees, migrants from the north, turned gold and red. They would remain leafless for a few weeks in deference to their heredity, then bud, leaf, and flower again. The autumn that is so brilliant in the north is hardly noticeable in the semitropics. It is only a pause in the cycle.

Life was returning but the alligator still had no food. Although the bass were growing rapidly, they were not large enough to eat, and the wood storks, who were big, managed to stay clear of her jaws.

She watched the small frogs swim and catch

insects. Cricket frogs, tree frogs, little glass frogs, pig frogs, and leopard frogs were food for the raccoons and birds, but not for her.

A crayfish that had lived all summer under the moist root of the cypress stalked to the pond bank and began picking up clumps of marl in its claws. These it placed in a pile. Digging and scooping, it cut itself a tunnel to the water and, backing down the tunnel, entered Sawgrass Hole, where it would feast on snails and dead fish. Other crayfish joined it.

At the end of October the river dropped still farther. The canal locks were opened to drain the land for the human farmers.

One morning the hungry reptile left her cave swimming slowly, for she was cold from the night air. She was headed for her beach to warm up in the sun. Suddenly she whipped her tail and lunged. A huge turtle had arrived in the pool. She slammed her jaws shut. Her long fast was over.

More turtles and big garfish were swimming into her hole from the drying glades.

When the moon of November rose, the alligator of Sawgrass Hole lay on her beach, a fixed smile on her face.

Bibliography

Barrett, Norma S. *Crocodiles and Alligators*. Mankato, Minn.: Crestwood House, 1984.

Bender, Lionel. *Crocodiles and Alligators*. Gloucester Press: 1988.

Cloudsley-Thompson, J. L. *Crocodiles and Alligators*. Milwaukee, Wis.: Raintree Publications, 1980.

Conant, Roger. *A Field Guide to Reptiles and Amphibians of Eastern Central North America*, The Peterson Field Guide Series. Boston: Houghton Mifflin, 1975.

George, Jean Craighead. *Everglades Wildguide*, Natural History Series. Office of Publications, National Park Service, U.S. Department of the Interior. Superintendent of Documents, U.S. Printing Office, Washington, D.C. 20402. Stock No. 2405-00497

Graham, Ada and Frank. *Alligators*. New York: Delacorte Press, 1979.

Hartley, William B. and Ellen. *The Alligator, King of the Wilderness*. Camden, N.J.: Thomas Nelson & Sons, 1977.

Moon, Cliff. *Alligators and Crocodiles in the Wild*. Wayland, 1984.

Morrison, Susan Dudley. *The Alligator*. Mankato, Minn.: Crestwood House, 1984.

Pruitt, Jim, and Nancy McGowan. *The North American Alligator*. Steck-Vaughn Co., 1974.

Scott, Jack Denton. *Alligator*. New York: G.P. Putnam's Sons, 1984.

Shaw, Evelyn. *Alligators*. New York: Harper & Row, 1972.

Zim, Herbert S. *Alligators and Crocodiles*. New York: William Morrow & Co., Inc., 1978.

Index